ENDLESS HOPE

A LOOK AT GLARING REALITY

PART 1

KEVIN EDWARD HAMLETT

ISBN 978-1-968970-61-1 (Paperback)
ISBN 978-1-968970-62-8 (Ebook)

Inquiries and Book Orders should be addressed to:
Leavitt Peak Press
17901 Pioneer Blvd Ste L #298, Artesia, California 90701
Phone #: 2092191548

To my faithful wife, Stephanie Hamlett, acknowledged mother and father, and to noted associates such as Raynard Harrington.

CONTENTS

ACKNOWLEDGMENTS

My appreciation is also extended to precious friends and colleagues such as the Docks and Mosely families, who believe in my literary efforts, and to any person who has inevitable obstacles, impediments, or setbacks.

A LOOK AT GLARING REALITY

Life stares us in the eye like some colossal cyclops with its irritable tentacles gripping us, thereby shaking and shaping our world. Some are grinded as sand while others are that perpetual milestone grinding life to sand. Which one are you as life fashions you into a hue? Are you, for instance, shining yellow, shaded gray, solid red, or even sky blue?

FOREWORD

My husband has a fervent desire to awaken the soul, encourage the heart, and strengthen the spirit. Moreover, life and eternity have meaning that is often misunderstood. To enlighten the mind seems overwhelming, yet it is captivating. In addition, understanding and overcoming circumstances bring future healing, thus providing ways to conquer upcoming obstacles. In a true sense, life's stages are in escapable. Through them, we have the opportunity to mature, face disappointments, and thereby obtain infinite hope. Furthermore, we have the opportunity to display courage, establish patience, and unfold the hidden identity that so eagerly awaits us, bringing out the beauty of love and hope in the midst of life's cloudy, uphill journey.

As we seek direction in life, patience and persistence bring about many unfulfilled dreams. More importantly, the fire in our souls ignites and inspires our surroundings, gaining the attention of those in need of an encouraging spark to brighten their outlook on life. Life is not meant to have never-ending dreariness, yet an examined life is radiant with God's help.

In the midst of our crises, our souls yearn usually to face the sunlight of rest. God knows the beauty of souls desiring everlasting joy, but in fact is crestfallen by crippling, cast iron burdens. In our deepest despair, however, there is a splendid and reachable hope out there.

So enjoy and draw inspiration from my husband's writings.

Stephanie Hamlett

ENDLESS HOPE

Even at the heart of our morbidity, we have the clear capacity
To move beyond the rumbling sea; Oh! Yes, as torturous as it may be;
We see beyond the big bronze burden—that shining sun above the
silver sea;
This benighted night from which those lads adore soon vanishes
from sullen shore;
Lest that eminent flash of hope rekindle more and more
With closing door;
A clarion sound from splendid mound,
Preserve and cherish that precious crystal
Allowing it to flourish
Thereby expanding in leaps and bounds.

—Kevin Hamlett

APHORISMS

On Maturity

One day an eaglet becomes an eagle; a cub becomes a full-grown fox, bear, or lion. So must a child become a full-grown man or woman.

On Disappointments

Every person faces some earmarks of disappointments when faced with reaching life's designated lot.

On Hope

It's night, but it's not midnight—don't give up! It's midnight, but it's not ten midnights—don't give up! It's a hundred midnights, but it's not a thousand midnights—don't give up! It's a thousand midnights, but not a million midnights—don't give up! Even if it is a million midnights—still don't give up!

On Life

On life's freeway, there's no guarantee of a pain-free way.

On Morality

You show me a man with muscles, and I'll show you a man with morals. Muscle boundness does not take precedence over moral soundness.

On Fame

Fame has a transient quality; it passes through the polluted air as smoke from a huge locomotive train, then it dissipates into thin air.

Thinking Success

Why squint in sorrow when you can squiggle in success?

Be Your Best

Why join a star-nose mole when you can be your own starting block in championship?

On Survival

A steamroller is for the rough roads while the smooth ways bear the mark of craftsmanship.

On Word of Mouth

Word of mouth is a seed that grows beyond the forest into any sea deck from island to island, country to country, nation to nation, and continent to continent.

On Anger

Concealed anger is as a time bomb waiting to explode; it may erupt at a clandestine meeting.

On Patience and Persistence

Patience and persistence outweighs panic and prattle.

On Courage

Though a man is haggard and haunted by the iceberg of crippling fear, he is invigorated or warmed by the sunrise of unfettered courage.

On the Heart

A heart may appear benign but be malignant.

On Gossip

Gossip is a filthy dumpster forming a fetid, foul odor.

On Pride

The inflated king served as a travesty of the majesty.

Our Lives

Our lives are as a bulletin board showing any existing form, figure, shape, configuration, contour, or profile.

On Complacency

Peace in absence of struggle is comfort and complacency.

On Evil Deeds

A villain's fraud deceives the perpetrator of the act as well as the receiver of the act, but the scoundrel's deeds will soon transpire. He is the hangman of his own destiny.

On Death

The bread of idleness can lead to the choke of death.

On the Writer

The pen or pencil serves as the writer's mouthpieces, the words are the writer's intended thoughts, and the readers are the writer's audience.

On Honesty

Honesty is painful at times, but it withstands all forms of hypocrisy or lies.

On Oppression

The master of the cage must open the cage door, lest the cage dwellers will be impelled to force it open and, thereby, destroy the cage.

On Truth

Truth is known alone on the throne, for it is never reconciled with evil.

Man on Puns

A man may pry a pun for fun but may not thumb the pun's drum.

On Life's Toughness

Life is sometimes tougher than bone marrow, but somehow one must face life's hardcoreness with perseverance, faith, courage, and confidence.

Irony of Helping Others

A strange irony in life is that we are so busy helping others that we at times do not have much time for our network of family and friends.

On Beauty

Ephemeral beauty may have an indelible imprint on a person's mind.

On Tobacco

He does not chew tobacco; he eschews it.

Man's Changing Moods

In the dramatic stages of life, many people have a polychromatic personality where they change colors, thereby acting each multiple scene.

Your Pedigree

One way to learn about your family tree is to have a lot of sons and daughters of your own. In each of those sons and daughters, there is a strange and remarkable trace of personality that once existed in your pedigree. In a sense, you see your ancestral line through your children and your children's children, so our own family research can also include examining traits of that in our current lineage.

Beyond Doubt

To say "never say you can't" really does stand as the perpetual turbo boost for the human species dynamic thrust.

Infinite Possibilities

You enter the peerless realm of infinite possibilities when you see beyond life's splendid royal mansions decked with a myriad of beauty wonder vineyards.

Mankind's Formula

The simple formula for desolate mankind is to never ever turn back and never ever look down but to ever look upward toward the Grand Stellar Triad.

Dead End

You enter a cul-de-sac when you believe that life enshrouded you with a huge black sagging sac.

Don't Choke the Dice

Add spice to life, but do not choke the dice, for life's medley of episodes makes you think twice; if not twice, then death will later find you as smothered stew in a boiling cauldron.

Strength to Silence

There is a remarkable strength to silence; in the realm of silence, you discover the great danger of waste in human haste.

INFINITE HOPE

Should my fatigued face flare with the bleak and battered markings
of share despair when a brilliant array of hope is yet out there?
Should I droop, drown, and frown especially when I have nothing
to fear?
Yes, the steep rugged mountain is so far ahead,
But I must keep walking and climbing until I reach the now seen
obscure end;
I am trampled not forsaken, for I arose and will not bend;
Life is sometimes a tumultuous sea "roaring" with no soothing breaks
in sight,
But I still see a crested rainbow in sight;
And will seize every opportunity to flee the dismal night;
And thereby move from crimson sunset toward glittering sunrise
soaring high in victorious flight,
Not submerging myself in the flood banks of despair;
Henceforth, I am here with renewed commitment to confront my
sporadic fear;
Yes, my hydra-headed fear is mutilated and lying prostrate;
I now gravitate toward triumph with relentless stride and intensified
pace;
So I affirm that my flooded face does not bear the dark, discordant
etchings of searing despair and fear as I run this blaring race!

FORGING AHEAD IN LIFE
WITH GREAT COMMITMENT

I

Life is sometimes a strange conundrum of misty-eyed recollections of the precious times spent with my inseparable loved ones.

Life is sometimes replete with deep shadowy exteriors of catastrophic uncertainty in which my best prerogative is to stand still.

Life is sometimes a vast amphitheater enclosed with piercing, boisterous winds.

Life is sometimes a grinding mill in which I am crushed utterly as fine harvest wheat.

Life is sometimes a foofaraw in which I am perceived as the nagging object of never-ending fuss, and thus I am left staggering at a tortuous foot hill—not bragging but, sadly, foot dragging.

II

At life's declinable moment of misfortune, I must forge ahead in life with great commitment and forthrightness.

I must pledge toward having earnest perseverance rather than becoming utterly pooped or played out.

I must pledge toward making a creative difference in life rather than being grossly indifferent toward life.

I must pledge toward lifelong efforts of gladly helping others rather than selfishly living it up with pernicious drugs and liqueur.

I must pledge not only toward reaching the glittering heavenly stars but also become sparkling celestial stars, thereby setting fresh innovative trails.

I must never forget that the sharp silver blades attached to the shining red-and-white windmill must henceforth whirl—so long as I languish not but greatly commit myself to reviving and energizing buoyantly into what is ultimately a crisp indomitable wind.

During life's rigors, grinning is not necessarily a sin—so long as I do not allow life's disappointments to make me become chagrin, but I must cease not to spin vigorously until I strongly sense a hurling win and, thereby, ultimately triumph over life's winding obstacles; but I must not stop until I breathe my last throbbing breath and cease from my last penetrating stare.

III

For I am now a brilliant California condor destined to soar toward majestic heights.

I am now esteemed as a Cabbage butterfly taking a fabulous flight into the fresh Spring Australian Rose Garden.

For I am now an unforgettable imperial moth taking a turbulent flight from the ghastly horrors of my devastating past soaring towards the pleasant splendors of the reconciling present.

So I must *forgive*

> *Forereach*
> *Forge*
> *Forevermore*
> *Favor*
> *Flavor*
> *From a*
> *Fathoming*
> *Feast that is worthy*
> *Fine food to the soul and body.*

HIDDEN IDENTITY

Why dost thou hide behind a fuzzy fountainhead of misplaced
    human identity?
Once a crystal clear springing stream of endowed human worth now
    gradually flows into a stagnating tributary of doubt;
Who at bay will detect these forlorn feelings?
Ever sinking into the dark density of unconsciousness,
Thereby becoming as the common muck rather than peerless
    glittering pearls of the Red Sea
Shaped as a pale protean conforming to every possible environment
    other than thy intended self;
Hard to locate the blending chameleon while rested upon grassy hills;
Difficult to range the file fierce fox while hiding inside of a huge cage
    in the Netherlands;
Amazingly difficult to pinpoint as it perceives itself as a flock of geese
    flying toward the tropical island of Argentina;
Not ready to stand solid as a mountain of courage, cringing by the
    anthills of cowardness;
Not ready to throw off sparks as a big dipper soaring above the black
    landmasses of clouds;
Sheltered inside a sinking hut void of conviction;
Never to blossom as an ostrich fern full bloom in Long Island, New
    York;
Despised, dejected, and degenerated are the uncultured weeds found
    inside a six-foot ditch;
How can this distorted self be emancipated from the gully of death?
When dost thou cease to be a goofy giggling gibbon swinging from
    dead and deserted trees?

Who can clear the poisonous path thou treadest from water hemlocks
to water lilies?
For no turning Thor will blow the whistle to awaken these thistles;
Aside from Greek mythology, only God through Christ sets thee at
liberty from the rushing spree;
Thou lantern of hope dost not have to be blocked by a sliding panel;
Horrifying phantoms of the past do not have to creep from some dim
sad dirty attic to fool and frighten thee.
Inside the upper room, a mantel surrounding the serene fireplace
hath warmth and grace, lifting thee up from thy gloomy face
and fate.

AN ECLIPSE OF THE HEART

Thy heart throbs in such rapid and illuminating joy,
Making the three-spine stickleback fish gladly swim the waters of
    Troy;
Echoing cheerful night songs that comfort the nocturnal bosom of a
    lonesome child
Producing bubbles of laughter having a loving heart that is tender
    and mild;
"Come here," sayest thou in such magnificent gaiety; watching the
    sly spider cunningly ensnare the flying flea;
Covered with silver webs as if signaling a life of wondrous bliss;
Glancing at the scintillating sun that absorbs the earth's fiber with
    such a passionate kiss;
Then soon that burning lantern of fire in obscured by the celestial
    shadow of the moon;
Feeling the current ecliptic impact of the sizzling sun darkens my
    bright heart by the moon's shadow of doom;
The burning zeal blazing inside my heart is now transformed into
    smoldering ashes of melancholy;
The sad thoughts of the obscured sun penetrates my broken heart
    with the lonesome words "sorry";
In passionate plea, my dark soul yearns to end the long night of this
    ecliptic sorrow;
Plunged into the bleak abyss of inner depression, I ask, "Will the sun
    come out tomorrow?"

CRESTFALLEN STAR

Oh! My plea, crestfallen star: "What has happened to thee?" Thou art close behind the nebula in outer space;

Once a luminous beauty king standing splendidly from the gargantuan galaxy is now dwarfed beneath a diffused mass of interstellar dust;

My saddened pause and plea—"What has happened to thee?"

Every now and then, I gawk as thou attemptest a breakthrough through the nebula's luminous patch,

Then I gape as the nebula's luminous patch is transformed into an utter dark spot in outer space;

Thy crestfallen city is light years away from the capital of growth and productivity;

So my perpetual plea is "What has happened to thee? Why is thy life snuffed in the Red Sea?"

THE TRAGIC DEATH
OF DEATH

I

Oh! Death prohibits thy monstrous tentacles from scratching my
    delicate earthly vessel;
Pulling one deathblow, making the daylight flicker then go out;
Pouring forth your oily hemlock as I drag along while you lock me
    in a tight wrestle;
Down I go but incessant death rattles don't mean I ended my route;
Conjuring up your death wishes, hoping I would soon die,
But my imperishable soul will leave you in a sorrowful cry.

II

Ushering in catastrophic winds with your deadly nightshade,
Making the evening stars wail and the dismal sky hang low;
Plaguing potatoes, mules, and fish, thereby producing horror as you
    pervade;
Moving as dark clouds of mosquitoes striking with your deathblow;
Holding up your silver sword after plunging the remains of a
    mutilated body;
Of whom was once a professional fighter in the Oriental art of karate.

III

At last, however, I stand over death as it sinks its dying hydra-headed
    body under the Great Babylonian River.

A previous victory won too soon brought your sudden doom;
Now I wear the crown reigning over your fragile trunk stripping out
    the large glands of your broken liver
Contrasting you and I naming dead Death "the Great Buffoon."

THE EARLY MORNING CHIME

Forewarning chimes sounding in the bleak bitter atmosphere,
    echoing sobering signals of alarm;
Producing tremors in those drenched with gripping fear, sounding
    steadily as rhythmic pendulums amid a huge farm;
In the industrial setting, traces of human bodies move mechanically
    toward the vast magnet of shops and factories;
Nevertheless, the sweet morning chime rings progressively;
Even the pallid human figures pause in their robotic strut, holding
    their thick phylacteries;
Resounding the barren and bleached valley effectively;
Ringing sharp sounds, awakening distant grizzly bear hibernating the
    trailless wood;
Stopping floating hammerheads while its sharp-edged sound arises
    beyond sea deck;
Developing into memorable cadences testifying to the radiant ark of
    universal good;
Refreshing the weary mind of the lonely owl sitting on the cold tree
    branch of neglect;
Coming from the spire as saints sing standing from benches of
    splintered wood;
"Our songs shall rise to thee," they sing, rendering the Creator
    magnificent respect:
Shall this impenetrable chime ever lose its monumental rank?
Silencing the celestial hierarchy ascending the ethereal bank.

THE EARLY MORNING FROST

On the windowpane lay frost;
Every minute ice crystal covered the windowpane;
As the snowstorm arrived no piece was lost;
Every crystalline material did not look the same;
Each fallen ice crystal formed small and large ice castings;
Yes, a splendid ice palace with bright silver-white mappings;
With an intricate mirror forming from the early twilight setting;
Who could fathom the mathematical formulas spinning the bright
    ice patterns into being?
Winter birds chuckle with their vibrant singing;
Out of the billowy white cloud lands pour forth bright snowdrifts
    that I enjoy seeing;
Boy! What a wonderful weather pattern of howling gale force winds
    and bright beams of snow;
Accumulating more frosted flakes on the window frames;
Producing jubilee from the youth desiring always to remain joyful as
    they age or grow;
Replenishing my heart, and my profound satisfaction sustains.

THE LIGHTHOUSE

Oh! Lighthouse-despondent mariners afar;
Bring him in, bring her in—emancipate them from that bloody scar;
Howling winds—lightning stroke;
Rising waters—broken spoke;
Sudden fear—don't lose hope!
Hear ye, oh, lighthouse, secure that sinking ship;
Beacon emanate from thee guiding thy velvet vessel from the dip.

IN A MATTER OF SECONDS

In a matter of seconds, there is a determining factor between me experiencing a rejuvenating life or facing a fatigable death, between me experiencing a transitory tragedy or seeing a perennial triumph, between me facing a jarring irreconcilable difference or meeting a smooth amicable tie, between me sobbing in a waning lamentation or lauding in a thriving jubilation, between me gasping in a horrid fear or embracing in an unflagging faith, between me executing a firm resolution or cringing in a feeble hesitation, between me having a brilliant conception or making a compelling execution, between me being among the ever obscure ordinary or being among the ever revealing phenomenal.

All of my intent, deed, and action are capsulated inside the delicate network of history. Oh yes, the flashing hand of life's seconds appear as a lustrous motion picture unraveling before my shocking eyes, displaying vividly the sometimes frantic or the more sane and humane features of my human existence.

In the ebb and flow of time's huge tide, what shall I decide?: Shall I joyfully live or tragically die? Shall I climb the smutty brick wall or forever soar toward the wonderfully deep blue sky?

GREAT MOMENT
OF TRIUMPH

That great moment of triumph soaring over every nagging woe;
Seeing vividly glittering star breaks—thunderous appeals over every
    battered foe;
The carved meandering road I sprint;
The luminous pin-cushioned cloud gives hint,
Then I hear a piercing clap of thunder;
This suspension raises attention—I'm not under;
Wailing glorious avail, I sail;
Boisterous winds, yet I prevail.

PRESSING INSIDE THE GATE

Don't hesitate, but press inside the gate;
Push! Push! Hey! Eagerly advance;
Walk, run, crawl, but don't wait;
Hop! Skip, lest you won't stand a chance;
Entering that serene gate as did others who did not procrastinate;
But with every effort clasped the pearly gate with a vigilant stance;
Yet in howling gale force winds, they made their advance.

THE SILVER TONGUE

The silver tongue is a vicious volcano spewing molten lava, obliterating
the most precious passionflower;
It is a sour silver sphinx snuffing the fresh bloodline from a gentle
maiden dying less than an hour;
It is a colossal Chimera drinking dry the Niger-Congo River;
It is a rough roaring rhinoceros destroying heaps of napalms, making
its Indian dwellers shiver;
Beware! A smooth venomous cobra stings its perceived prey when
idle bystanders least expect;
Oh no! The black albatross travels with my message from north,
south, east, and west, for whom can detect?
Help! Help! Tapeworms creep from my kitchen cabinet, crawling
quietly into the open meowing mouth of my black cat;
Watch that eager beaver by placing a cap on its trap…zap!

DON'T WANE THE WAIL

As the growling and the howling winds make an upward sail, don't
    wane the wail;
Wail and sail steadily over the meandering trail;
Let your mournful cry be heard, intensifying over the walloping wall
    flowers;
Let your lament be heard, increasing over the hammerhead sharks
    that devour;
Let your untainted wail prevail over the mighty torrents that shower;
Disseminate, don't dissipate;
Your incessant wail will burst the serpent's prehensile tail;
An unfailing wail will bail you from the boisterous gale,
And hence sail "The Victorian Ship" over the rumbling wale;
Run toward the crested metal;
Run-agate from any treacherous snake;
A jovial wail brings you over the nettle into a gladly approved and
    gloriously awaited date;
So let not the wail wane;
You cannot fail but prevail;
Any moment now determinedly mark the spectacular countdown;
Remain firm, fervent, thus igniting a flame as you receive a five-star
    crown.

FIRE

Fire burns to ashes the Massachusetts Barn;

Fire burns through the thick pine log in Idaho;

Fire blazes through every cog and motor of the machinery in the Wyoming Factory;

Fire enrages a bulldog to claw his teeth into the damsel's thumb;

Fire ignites a man to plunge a knife into his chest, pronouncing him dead at the Jamaica Scene;

Fire causes Nicky to study science with alacrity and, hence, pass her exam with flying colors;

Fire spurs a vigilante of veterans into resisting a recalcitrant mob who later succumbs to the veteran's appeal;

Fire consumes any embrasure and, thus, torments any human soul;

Fire purifies any embrasure and, thus, ennobles any human spirit;

Fire discharges blue, black, red, and orange flames of paradoxical tendencies in whatever or whomever it embodies.

WAGON WITHOUT WHEELS

On the Mediterranean Sea,

I see in Morocco a golden wagon without wheels;

Oh! How the mustang pushes, pulls, and plows, but the wagon will
    not yield;

At first the mustang wails, then it releases a Wahoo as the wagon
    becomes a waif cast upon the Mediterranean Sea;

With staggering achievement, the black mustang gallops and on
    hind's feet brushes through the Morocco land gay and free.

A VACANT MIND IN NEED OF GOD'S GRACE

A mind once clothed in transcendent brightness is now like mere
jetsam or flotsam drifting on the sea.

A mind having the cosmic capacity to reach the Third Heaven has
now descended into a vast vulnerable valley of hopelessness.

A mind wherein calm reservoirs of peace once collected is now
obstructed by the turbulent storms of darkening sin.

Alas! Do we yet believe that the binding power of human intellect
supersedes the cohesive, all-knowing power of God?

Do we yet believe that the wide range of scientific discoveries
supersedes God's power of creating something out of nothing?

Do we yet believe that the earth's intricate fabric was once weaved
into existence through our very own steady ingenious thinking?

Think of the huge mountains kissing the sky like an aircraft rising to
great stature.

Think of the miraculous flow of a small gentle stream feeding into a
yet more peaceful tributary.

Think of the molten lava powerfully erupting from a volcano, causing
an explosively violent destruction on earth.

How much more forceful will God arrive with His volcanic wrath
heating this world?

So let us consider the inexpressible depth of God's omnipotence,
realizing that we are like unarmed grasshoppers in need of
God's great grace.

O Lord Our Lord, how excellent is thy name in all the earth!
—Psalm 8:9

SHORT FLIGHTS

A sudden flight into the dismal night;
With transient stellar sparkling in the night, tawdry pearls;
Dreary worlds suddenly vanish into the thin purple garments of
      oblivion;
No more than a fuzzy whim or caprice that is subject for suspicion;
Hammered and nailed for further inspection;
With the detective's piercing eye finding the detection;
Bound, breakable, lost, dross;
Squealing into its flimsy source;
For it's a shallow scallop doomed in a dam or a flighty flimflam
      known as a hollow sham;
So why take a sudden flight into the dismal night?

THE BEAUTY OF LOVE

The beauty of love is that it stretches beyond our fragile textile of foibles or faults.

Though love perceives our many frailties, this potent, powerful, peaceful force bridges us into a mutual network of unwavering appreciation, loyalty, dedication, and commitment.

Yes! Its architectural beauty is more far reaching than the majestic royal castles of Spain or the gargantuan buildings glaring the New York City day skies or the dazzling bridges connecting the bright arteries and veins of Chicago City night.

Its thick and solid tapestry is too profound for any mortal vessel to fathom.

It will leave average scientists cringed under "Sweet Harlem" potholes with their tongues sticking out—panting for fresh air.

Though they are exasperated, yet they are also at awe at love's mysterious beauty.

It leaves average historians dumbfounded or confounded under their very own rubbish of historical collections found in Russia.

It leaves anthropologists gaping in their studies of…but yet anthropologists' arms quake in Egypt at love's mysterious force.

Its prodigious landmark is what adorns us with manifold garments, hence placing us toward the center of our very own emotions, feelings, intelligences, and spirits.

'TIS BEAUTY

'Tis beauty harmonizing spectacular shades of gray and black;
'Tis beauty soothing my heart with philharmonic cords of satisfaction
    and happiness;
'Tis beauty uprooting any dark clay of anxiety in me, thereby rushing
    forth with an inimitable wellspring of rest in me;
'Tis beauty illuminating throughout every red ribbon, holding that
    brilliant ruby, jasper, and pearl together;
Such splendid beauty is in thee and throughout thee!

TROUBLE IN THE DEN

Oh! There's trouble in the den, my friend;
Lions, tigers, scorpions, and snakes rail at me;
Enthralled by slimy sneers and gins of creeping creatures in the den;
I run, and then I sink while the Norwegian elkhound stares at me;
Pitch dark with numb thumb in an abyss;
Neither phloxes nor myrtles nor muntjacs in view;
Ravening ground beetles snoot snoop-life risk;
Rather zigzag and climb a ziggurat seeing Mesopotamian blue.

THE FLICKERING FLAME

By the velvet window pane;

I do see the same flickering flame;

That doth not ignite from its faint remain;

Transcending the ecstatic joy of the full golden moon;

But does not compare to the sun's piercing stare, only plunging ground in swoon;

Oh! Fainting flame in the windowpane, please ignite to luminous heights;

Blooming daylight into gloomy rooms of automatons ignoring "the woos of million midnights!"

THE MISSING SCREW

That missing screw not in joint;
Places a wooden frame off the point;
Weakens that paved foundation;
Unfastens a ceiling fan, thereby increasing in vibration;
Untightens the delicate fabric of countless generations;
Corrupts the moral framework of endless corporations;
Scatters huts, tribes, villages, and nations;
That missing screw sears or mars a source;
Finding and binding the screw muzzles the mouth of the horse.

ODE TO THE CLOUDS

Oh! Those clouds decorating the heavens like fluorescent lamps
With magnificent blends of brilliant beams shining through celestial
    cotton;
Providing the naked heavens with intricate pillory ramps;
Ascending each dimensional cloud chamber, leaving splendid layers
    of silvery cotton;
Swirling evangelical spheres making human minds transcend
    manacles of time;
Crystallizing into thick coatings of dense fog;
Formulating huge cloud lands ascending to unreachable depths of
    cloud nine;
Releasing mighty torrents from your cosmic catalog;
Veiling the deadly future of political buffoons chanting cloudless
    words of deception;
Dimming the mirrors of people obsessed by furtive charms;
Billowing as from giant steamrollers erasing ruinous particles in your
    direction;
Emitting thunderous groans setting off people's car alarms;
Gently moving methodically from one stratosphere to another;
Always adorning the heavens with your soft beautifully layered cover.

BE READY TO FACE
THE SHINING SUN

Your upward hill journey has just begun, but be ready to face the
    glittering sun;
Tired…weary…perplexed…downtrodden… Don't take the smooth
    way for fun;
For your upward hill journey has just begun;
Look to the black widow spider whose web has been spun;
It spins diligently in angular momentum in the nocturnal cool day;
Extruding its web along the pastoral way;
Bridging its sticky web along the thin stems of a loblolly pine tree
As the radiant sun projects binding web with beautiful brilliancy;
Whether summer, winter, spring, or fall;
A lesson from one, a lesson to all:
Let your job be well done,
And thus be ready to face the scintillating sun!

BEAUTY FORMED WITHOUT HUMAN HANDS

Thou mortal being scintillates as crystals on the windowpane;
Thou art more splendid than the glorious fountainhead with the
    shining rainbow on its left side;
Thou art more admirable than the row of bristle cone pines native to
    the Western United States;
Thou art also decked with a wonderful interior of peerless sweetness,
    unforgettable kindness, and reminded gentleness;
The Maker only designs such capacious beauty formed without
    human hands.

ARISE

Arise crestfallen ones,
Leaping and reaching for that gleaming star!
Thus, mounting and surmounting—dear, touch that luminous sun!
Neither crashing nor splashing into the surging tidal waves of stark
    despondence
But, rather, dashing or splashing into the fresh reservoir of resurgence,
Setting foot on new and steady shores—never to remain the same,
Adding meaningful zest into your depository bank of life—a special
    collection stored for safekeeping
As a ringing reminder not to, at once, smear into the shallow grounds
    of stagnation.
Left as shaded fossils found beneath an ambiguous edifice later
    discovered by scientists
Only to stir wonder and awe kept within the confines of
    anthropologists to cherish
But replenishing the earth as reoccurring sparks that ripple across
    the sea
With its increasing wavelike motions, thereby reverberating
    throughout the world.

—Kevin Hamlett

JAYBIRDS

Two jaybirds sing in the sizzling summer heat,
Their perpetual symphonies soothe the rumbling ridges in McCarthy
    Pond;
Look an hour later.
Two jaybirds
String sonorous songs
From pointed pine tree
To pointed pine tree.
Look an hour later
Inside the night's thick dome reverberates the pleasant melodies only
    found in
Its transient and nocturnal form.
And lost in the vast web of time, two jaybirds forever gone and
    forgotten.
Or
Are they forever gone and forgotten as they remain cherished almost
    endlessly by human memories?
Yet a continuum of talk of these sweet, remarkable jaybirds exists
    around the family dinner table,
Around Barnes and Noble Book Stores
And even among special restaurants such as Red Lobster, Longhorn,
    and Olive Garden.
Yes, something that may seem so infinitesimal in value has
    monumental meaning and depth
Set only for a sensitive humanity to marvel over.

—Kevin Hamlett

THERAPEUTIC ANGER

Therapeutic anger forces me to confront the raging tidal banks
flooding my soul.
This creative anger compels me to transcend cowardice, thus
displaying courage.
Though I'm downright tired of this nagging thistle, my torrid
indignation produces passionate sweat
Transforming any cumulous thunderheads of anxiety into a cool,
crisp, cloudless oasis of peace.
So let the dreaded winds that travel along the coast of New Jersey,
Which formulate the waters into rushing ripples and waves come;
So let the soon forgotten splendid sunlight hide beneath the thick
clouded days come;
So let the generated heat from the hot pizza burn the roof of my
mouth come;
One by one, each obstacle is seared into ashes as specks floating upon
the shores of Asia
Through the creative outpouring of therapeutic anger.

—Kevin Hamlett

THERAPEUTIC LAUGHTER

Therapeutic laughter is as a wellspring of cool water cleansing the
    vital organs from bacteria contributing to strain and stress;
It releases the burdens of the mind through a tonic cheer;
It revitalizes a staggering soul toward an unassailable poise;
Why, it even causes one to walk unattended across the narrowest
    bridge in Tennessee
And walk amid soaring billows in London!
Face vituperations void of fury and venom as a stroke of lightning
    portrays itself as a hammer fist
Pounding against the delicate drenched branches of a hackberry tree
    of Georgia;
A moderation of laughter can keep piercing anger at bay,
And find great joy in facing the uncertainties of the day;
A healthy sense of humor helps one change from a sag to a sprint
    along life's winding pathway.

—Kevin Hamlett

PRIDE'S WAY

Oh, thou flourishing mortal with healthy sinews and muscles now
    set afoot on Mount St. Helens
With a Herculean pose and an enlarged brazen fist
Elevated with a definitive for thou "proclaimed" Olympian stature.
Enchanting cruel and seething remarks toward any one perceived as
    foe and enemy;
Intimidating tender mothers codling their babies while cringing in
    tiny huts,
Raging at other mortals refusing to abide by thy decrees,
But thou lingerest inside any tunnel and cave as a pernicious banana
    spider,
And believe thy "prestige" hurls into a powerful limitless trajectory.
Yes, thou secretest venom from thy silver tongue. Thy disposition is
    inimical.
Thy presence is transitory. Thou thinking art delusional.
Yet thou say: I'm mighty. I'm mighty. I'm mighty.
What flaring, sheer folly.

DARE TO DREAM

Part I

Dare to dream beyond the roaring seashores and beyond the giant Odyssey that wavers from the steady course, almost being swallowed up by fierce winds and waters.

Dare to dream beyond St. Helens that rumples and, thus, belches up billows of smoke as a gargantuan sea monster that thinks she has a coup de grace against Hercules.

Dare to dream beyond the vast valley of death that wiggles its tongue as if to pull you in as a mammoth damaging suction tube.

Dare to dream beyond the hideous Medusa with her ghastly head of writhing serpents and, hence, reach beyond the magnificent pyramids of Egypt.

For a dream is but a creative, lovely sight that will soon come to pass if the dreamer diligently works toward manifesting what he believes is worth seeing.

So keep dreaming until the piercing radiant sunlight melts through the large sheets of white and grey ice, thereby unveiling that tranquil blue ocean.

Yes! Dare to dream beyond the ocean's circumference into another continent, into another island, into another mainland—whether it will be in Antarctica, Asia, Australia, Europe, North America, or South America.

Dare to dream as the sweeping message shines into a distinguished crescent-shaped moon throughout the thick fog of the night, thereby producing an indelible imprint upon every night dweller, with a shining light that radiates throughout the scope of life itself or even beyond the span of time.

—Kevin Hamlett

PREPARATION FOR BATTLE

Crisp cool breeze, crimson honey sap trees, solemn sleepless soldiers await blooming battle at hand;

Fine firm fort at bay, Garfield, gallant general five-star display, outside drum boy baton directs band;

Piercing, pounding sound summoning loyal military subjects, thereby stamping magnetic feet upon solid ground;

Yet disenchanted military maverick objects drum boy sound, seething flare—"General grey hound!";

Utter anger, pale general questions forlorn soldier, "Why did thou not respond to nearby drum?"

Victor replies, "I could not beckon to nearby drum. Basis of my conscience made it irresistible to shun;

I suppressed an inner drum, displaying discordance...battle fatigue. Why me?... Why not me?"

Clear-cut program I need to perceive for me;

A cold-blooded massacre rumbling troubled sea;

Blameless infants sob tireless echoes of woes behind mammoth mountain of debris,

Pallid father grasps only priceless portrait as his son's grim remains lingering murky sea;

Bustling maimed mother, withered arm pointing toward charring red-bricked chimney;

Smog and soot spew continuously from uncanny sky...sudden wail protruding lips—huff puff—churning sea;

Rubble stemming ruined edifices, shambled bungalows, vivid memory,

Once still earth now quivers in dread...then shakes in sorrow...
now swirls in turmoil from continued consumption of noxious
machinery;
A seething cauldron ready to explode as dispatch bearer bends frail
knee to flee;
As flames engulf, meager maiden runs toward listless mulberry tree;
Is there any news on any hemisphere that will not capture this all-
too-dreadful catastrophe?
Inexplicable, endless, ubiquitous...salvo...bravo reign...bombs
bursting tree to tree;
Sea to sea and so far, no sign of glee to see;
Why did troubled general Garfield confront Victor dual in battle
front, combating against himself and forced battle Royal,
destroying countless of lives...you see?
No... No... Not Victor, one of many not foot note in relief;
As rustling winds wrestled against fresh ashes from napalm, he did
not waver from belief;
For he serves as an exemplary and legendary hero, thus leaving a
remarkable trail, serving as an ingrained Inky cap, a shiny cream
cup, or a special sweet maple leaf, thus peerless from the bleak
crusted Maiden hair tree;
Yes "preparation for battle" involves psychological armory serving as
a bullwhip against human creed or irrationality.
Amid turmoil, there is a citadel of hope to draw a well of life with
consistency, harmony, and liberty.
A remembered song artist named Marlo Thomas, in her cherished
song, "Free to Be...You and Me," recaptures some of the
growing relevancy of freedom and self-identity:

There's a land that I see where the children are free
And I say it ain't far to this land from where we are
Take my hand, come with me,
Where the children are free
Come with me take my hand,
And we'll live
In a land where the river runs free

In a land through the green country
In a land to a shining sea
And you and me are free to be You and me (1–12)
(Published by Thomas, Marlo. *Free to Be You and Me*. Bell Records.
May-July 1972)

May we awaken to a new land, cherished and renewed by the
promises awaited to everyone who envisions this real possibility of
that glorious and forthcoming reality;

Let the beaming sun permeate throughout every sunless and moonless
nightfall, illuminating dreary valley and bleak sea as its fascinating
brightness extends yet toward another breathtaking apogee.

—Kevin Hamlett

(Note: The origin of song I can remember hearing at P. S. 132/Ralph
J. Bunche Elementary School in Queens, New York during 1976 to
1980s.)